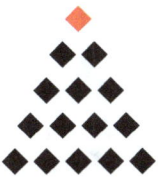

~enriched~
~uplifted~
~branched~
~rooted~

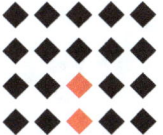

The Campaign
for
Red Door

You had me at meta.

A new, sustainable, and powerful model (but not the only model, of course) for arts agency and prosperity will be ushered in by the participart. I hope you will follow Red Door and become a participart. It is different than being an audience member or a spectator. A participart is an integral player in the vitality of communities enriched by artistic contributions to human life.

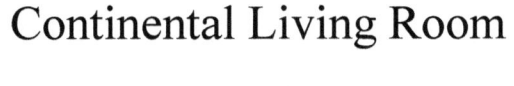

Continental Living Room

Continental Living Room is Red Doors in neighborhoods all over this country.

Red Doors are Neighborhood Catalysts and Cosmic Third Places.

Red Doors are MetaHouses, bringing in the qualities of ecumencialism, conversation, and cross-fertilization.

They are Cosmic Third Places because they are customizable, adaptable arts-infused common spaces and gathering places that are sites of learning, collaboration, respite, conversation, healing, meditation, imagination, inspiration, action, connect, and neighborliness. And they are Neighborhood Catalysts because of everything I just said.

Once upon a time in American, frontier towns demonstrated their credibility and hipness by having a college, then a railroad, then an opera. In the 1970s and 1980s, the wish was for a research park or economic development zone or a huge, new factory. Then it was to be a city of creators.

Red Doors will bring vitality, reinvigoration, and vibrancy to communities by way of enlivened and prosperous neighborhoods.

Red Doors, at least for awhile, will be the new "it."

When I was a featured speaker at Dubuque's inaugural humanities festival, organized by the Dubuque (Iowa) Museum of Art, I spoke on new visions of practice for arts and humanities and new sites/places where these practices could take place. During the question-and-answer section for my talk, an art history professor, somewhat perplexed by my perspective and insight, asked a question as a statement.

"What you're talking about," he said, "could take place in a bowling alley."

Bingo, I thought.

Red Door will be a novel and innovative site for arts and humanities. And I can imagine the same for a bowling alley. In fact, Wayward Social is a brand new bowling alley in Marshalltown, Iowa that by design or by accident is an unorthodox site for arts and humanities that will become an inspiration such places to become orthodox sites for arts and humanities.

This is why the cover of this book features a picture of the Times-Republican, the community's newspaper, featuring an article on Wayward Social.

Red Door will open floodgates for new artistic conversations and community enrichments.

This book belongs to the trilogy, **<u>Operation Standing Room Only</u>**, which will introduce the following concepts to the world:

Artober Caucus
Red Door Neighborhood Catalyst
Adrian's International Day for the Arts and Humanities
Cultural Substrate

The books in the trilogy are:

<u>Continental Living Room</u>
<u>Across the Fruited Plain</u>
<u>7-Spot Crown</u>

Continental Living Room

Pioneering (Arts-Based) Vectors
for
Personal Enrichment,
Community Building,
and
Societal Learning;
or
the
Making of MetaHouse

Patrick Muller

Other books by Patrick Muller

Healthcare Communication
A Rhetorical Handbook

I can cure your cancer with this poem
Medicine as Language and Story
(written as author: belfort wunder)

Across the Fruited Plain
Nourishing Cultural Substrate and Transcendent Societies

7-Spot Crown
Mapping of the Art Genome

This edition is not illustrated (for the sake of practicality and expediency.) Future editions will be. In the meantime, feel free to add your own doodles.

I.

This is a two-part exploration.

The first part takes place in this book and examines Red Door, which has its own two parts.

Red Door is 1. the prototypical gathering space, laboratory, and headquarters for Red Door franchises; and 2. the home of red dor, a 6000-square foot living destination *p*Painting.

Red Door will be a MetaHouse, a neighborhood catalyst, and cosmic third place.

More so, Red Doors will strive to be relevant and sustainable and so will be agents of economic development for a community

The second part takes place in the next book, Across the Fruited Plain, which defines "cultural substrate," and suggests the substrate's nourishment will help the arts to flourish everywhere, not just in cosmopolitan centers. More ubiquitous and substantive arts presence will facilitate personal enrichment, community building, and societal learning.

Which takes us back to the first part: Red Doors will be neighborhood and regional sites of new models for personal enrichment, community building, and societal learning.

So really, this is a *Two-Part Plan to Reinvigorate/Stabilize the Arts and Make Empathic & Critical Thinking the DNA of the American Soul.*

II.

Red Doors will be commercial spaces with compositions shaped by local communities. In some part, they will be emporiums with different mixes of retail and services offerings. Of course, Red Doors will always be stealth museums, subtle art galleries, gathering spaces, community centers, and enrichment portals.

So Red Doors will eventually bring in more revenue than expenses and be profit centers. But to get them started, especially the prototypical Red Door -- which will be the headquarters and a laboratory for community building and audience engagement -- we will employ crowdsourcing to get the project going through its first couple of phases.

We will implement a new concept in crowdsourcing called Usage Fee Philanthropy.™ Usage Fee Philanthrophy™ (UFP™) is a simple and modest but powerful ask.

Nowadays, when people purchase a ticket to a performance, there can be as many as five usage fees. There can be a ticket handling fee, an order fee, a fee for the ticket processing company, a building fee (to help renovate the organization's facility), and even a box office fee (to pay the organization's box office staff, though shouldn't that operational expense be priced into what the organization charges for tickets?) If tickets to a show costs $25, and two tickets are purchased, that $50 purchase can surprisingly/shockingly balloon to $65.

Here is how this breaks down:

Two tickets @ $25 each	50.00
$2 handling fee X 2 tickets	4.00
$3 order fee	3.00
$4 online ticket company processing fee	4.00
$2 box office staff fee	2.00
$2 building renovation fund fee	2.00
Total	**65.00**

Usage fees in this example boost the price of the tickets thirty percent. This may seem excessive but last year I paid a thirty-five percent premium in usage fees. Five to ten percent would be minimum in most cases. In many cases, fifteen to twenty percent would be the norm.

Riffing off this reality of usage fees is how we will fund the first phases of this Red Door project. In the example above, the usage fees charged on the vast majority of online ticket orders today is the ticket handling fee, the order fee, and the processing company fee. (4+3+4) = $11

$11 is both nominal, not a great some of money in the larger scheme of things, and monumental; it's 22% of this $50 order!!! With Usage Fee Philanthropy™ crowdfunders can take a nominal sum (we normally will ask for $6-8, sometimes $17) and turn it into a monumental, phenomenal outcome: creating the headquarters for Red Door and launching the first handful of Red Door satellites in neighborhoods around the country and nourishing the cultural substrate (which will help bring the essentiality of the arts into everyone's daily lives.)

Artober Caucus (discussed later in this book) will be the first and main Usage Fee Philanthropy™ initiative to get Red Door moving. The cultural substrate will be funded through a "usage fee" initiative called Adrian's Day: International Arts and Humanities Day. "Usage fee" initiatives are part of a network called Badges of Meaning. Crowdfunders can collect both virtual and physical badges to fund Red Door's first phases and nourish the cultural substrate.

Artober Caucus for Red Door will be the first Badge of Meaning. Participarts, defined soon, will be able to collect virtually and/or physically numerous Badges of Meaning that will help fund the initial and future phases of the Red Door project.

III.

     We need to rethink, if we want to truly actualize our potential as a species, the notion of cultural events. Reading a book, listening to a song on the radio, consuming a blog, enjoying a fine dinner, attending a play or dance or opera, attending a reading or lecture, attending a concert, visiting an art exhibition or gallery, visting a library or bookstore, visiting a museum or historical site or botanical garden or zoological garden, attending a party or any social moment with friends -- these are much more than entertainments, escapes, diversions, social markings; these are much more than something to do. Every activity like this is always an occasion for learning, enrichment, growth, and actualization. And it is always an occasion to sustain or reinvigorate enrichment that has already occurred. Making most moments of life occasions for learning and reinvigoration ought to be your first guidepost whatever ideology and tribes you subscribe to.

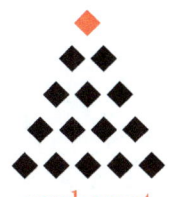

~exuberant~
~explorative~
~involved~
~engaged~
~substantive~

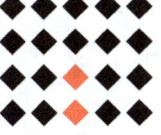

IV.

Breasts. Vaginas. Clitorises. Penises. Testicles. Asses. Tongues. Lips. Beer. Wine. Booze. Sex.

Too many people, when they see the hashtag #art or the word art, they just keep on rolling.

We need to talk about art. Yes, even you need to talk about art. Art is the prerequisite way of human knowing. Art is as essential to daily life as good nutrition, exercise, self-care, conversation, learning, purpose, and social connection.

We need to talk about art for a bit, but if I mention art, you will go ho hum and turn away.

So, in this instant, I won't talk about art. I will talk about breasts, vaginas, clitorises, penises, testicles, asses, tongues, lips, beer, wine, booze, sex. Welcome to the conversation.

V.

I realize you may not like my take on art. I'm not saying it is the entire definition of art. But if we want the arts to flourish and take their integral role in human society and daily lives -- no longer seen as a luxury or as something extraneous, something that so many can brush off; if we want the arts to reach their potential at interpreting and mentoring the human condition; then you need to buy into this take on the arts for this small moment.

VI.

Decoration, entertainment, escape, diversion, proclivity, trophy taking, and social marking are no more art than a Twinkie® is good nutrition.

Decoration, entertainment, escape, diversion, proclivity, trophy taking, and social marking are no more art than five minutes of party badminton is a good exercise workout.

VII.

Art is threatening to so many because it is inquiry and investigation. It pokes at the sutures and palpates the scaffolding dissects the social constructions that prop our ideologies, tribes, and societies up. It pulls the proverbial Oz curtain back on our assumptions to show us what is cooking.

What is more threatening and destabilizing and delirious to the insecure, corrupt, power-hungry, dishonest, self-esteemless, and/or underperforming than that.

But those inquiries and investigations are great resources and power for humans to actualize their potential.

VIII.

More so than asking our ideologies and assumptions to articulate and prove themselves, art threatens in a much more fundamental way: it insists that we are substantive.

Some artists become so skilled at their production that they can whip out a song or a painting or a poem in seemingly no time at all. That is an illusion. A work-of-art leans upon genealogies of experience, perspective, expertise, and practice that extend back for as long as the artist has been an artist, for as long as the artist has been human, for as long as the artist has been alive.

We are used to pop renditions of art that stroke our shallow, unreflective assumptions about ourselves and keep us mired in face-value, vapid analyses of our experiences. (This is not to say that most popular art cannot have incisive value; but there is much popular art that is deliberately manipulated not to have incisive value.) We get into the practice of consuming art that gives us immediately recognizable, comfortable, and familiar narratives. We develop an aversion, if not a repulsion, to any art that makes us put in effort, insists that we collaborate to tease out meaning, and expects to do a deeper, broader, and sustained dive into processing the creative stimuli.

We want art that affirms our narrow, shallow, and quite often rigid processing of ourselves, others, and the world. And we can get down right nasty or apathetic if art asks us to do the opposite. But that is exactly what art does: offers us the opportunity to broaden our narrows, deepen our shallows, and flex our rigidity -- all the while increasing the duration of these impacts. This is substance.

Art is always a moment of learning, a moment of emotional-cognitive life. Art always invites us to fire up our minds, actualize our human potential (that is accessed only broadly, deeply, flexibly, and enduring), regale in this exuberance, and so ignite our transcendence.

IX.

Art is entrance into <u>meta-analysis</u>: learning the intent behind a human response to a task or stimulus rather than just regurgitation an ideologically pigeon-holed response to that task or stimulus. So with intent of the response rather than ideology of the response, art opens an individual up to the <u>ethnosphere</u>: the dynamic sum total of all the human responses to a particular task or response in human existence. Now the individual has that entire universe at hir disposal. That is hir toolit. A myriad of responses and not just the suffocating one or two that an ideology allows. So art gives us a really sophisticated and appropriate blueprint to frame and process the world (elevated beyond ideology or orientation): meta-analytical ethnospheric understanding.

When I look at the upper levels of models of human emotional-cognitive development, I see mindsets that begin to approach meta-analytical ethnospheric understanding. Thus, <u>the arts are emotional-cognitive lift.</u>

X.

Tools are abstractions. Languages are abstractions. Memories and expertise and knowledge and equations and models and formulae are abstractions. Painting on cave walls is an abstraction. Human beings emerge from their capacity for abstraction. When human beings started painting on cave walls, diving full-frontally into abstraction farming and metaphor wrangling, they became human.

So, when humans started making art, that is really when they became human.

So, art is not just one way of human knowing; <u>the arts are the prerequisite way of human knowing.</u>

First art, then human.

XI.

Humans are constantly bombarded with stimuli and tasks of living they must complete each day. Humans make sense of these stimuli and form responses to these tasks through their capacity for language. Sense-making and responses happen with abstractions, metaphors, symbols -- humans are really the symbolic species -- myths, interpretations and stories.

Each human moment is a performance. Sadly, most humans most of the time choose a very limited and usually a coerced set of dialogue, costumes, roles, and interactions to interface with this moment. But humans have all kinds of stories available to them to respond to the moments of life.

Human life is a life of stories; and the arts are the proprietary way of knowing for stories. <u>The arts, treasure chest full of stories, become the palette for enriching, fortifying, and reinvigorating one's life.</u>

XII.

    The arts can look at a phenomenon through many facets. The arts are a wellspring of perspective and a great, inexpensive resource for communities. The arts can paint open windows when there are closed doors. The arts offer polyfaceted insights. <u>The arts are community thought leaders</u>, and a wise, empathic community utilizes them as such.

XIII.

Humans are not humans because they breathe, eat, drink, piss, shit, work, and have sex. Humans are humans because they farm abstractions, wrangle metaphors, make sense of their stimuli, interpret facts, imagine things, and tell stories. Humans' cultural life is as much of their definition of survival and prosperity definitions as anything biological.

More so.

The cultural life is not extraneous or expendable. Humans cannot not value paintings and dances and poems when people do not have enough to eat. It is never an either/or condition; it is both/and. And even when people are starving, they will feed themselves with stories and songs.

<u>The arts are baseline and integral and core to the human condition</u>.

XIV.

The arts are as essential to daily life as good
nutrition, exercise, self-care (meditation, reflection,
relaxation), learning, conversation, and social connection.

XV.

Because of their vast treasure of story, insight, perspective, meaning, empathy, analysis, and understanding, the arts are teacher, mentor, elder, collaborator, neighbor, friend, citizen, family member, even lover.

XVI.

◆ The arts are emotional-cognitive life.

◆ The arts are the prerequisite way of human knowing.

◆ The arts become the palette for enriching, fortifying, and reinvigorating one's life.

◆ The arts are community thought leaders.

◆ The arts are baseline and integral and core to the human condition.

◆ The arts are as essential to daily life as good nutrition, exercise, self-care, learning, conversation, and social connection.

◆ The arts are teacher, mentor, elder, collaborator, neighbor, friend, citizen, family member, even lover.

XVII.

I give these sections numbers, like this one is 16. This suggests a chronology, a linearity, a rigidity, a certainty, a dogma. It's really just a, likely ephemeral, tactic to organize and parse my thoughts into something remotely cogent and coherent.

Any one of these vignettes could be the one that resonates most with the reader. And the reader can interface with them in any order, in many combinations of order. My works are always evolving conversations, not frozen scripts.

I hope in few editions of this book, these numbers do not exist and so a linearity is not so strongly suggested and harshly framed.

XVIII.

The arts to artists are techniques to explore and challenges (light, color, foreground, melody, plot, rhythm, and so on) to meet. And we can understand how artists are content with that and never feel compelled to venture any farther.

In the hands of human and the world, however, the arts are so much more. The arts are perspective, insight, story, interpretation, sense-making, empathy, analysis, learning, and understanding.

The arts must interface with the world, but that interface is far too important to leave to artists, curators, gallerists, art historians, and cultural center administrators.

XIX.

In a great sense, the artist and the work-of-art do not even matter. Well, of course, they do, but they are really raw materials. Art happens not when an artist creates a work-of-art. A work-of-art begins when it is taken out into conversation and consideration with humanity and the world.

XX.

If you plan to offer a concert or a dance or a play or a reading or a lecture or an exhibition and you do not also plan for multiple portals and layers for conversation, consideration, and other enlightening and enriching interfaces, then you are squirting eggs and sperm on sizzling hot, parched rock.

I am that something more.

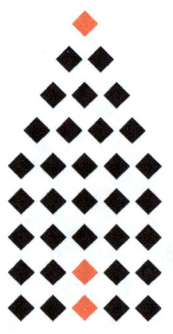

I am a participart.

XXI.

As you can tell, I believe the arts are essential to daily life and to one's actualization as a human being. I say this because I think it true and because we need to nurture pervasive and fervent support for the arts. If the arts want to prosper -- to stop, in so many places, being an afterthought; if the arts, as they must in so places, want to stop begging for funds and stop living on the edge of fragility and neglect; then they need to broaden, deepen, intensify, and extend their audiences.

But audience is not really what we need. I want to retire that concept. Audience is too spectator, too "please titillate me," too "give me comfort and familiarity and pleasantry," too passive. Audience, even though most audience members will deny it, is too fickle and superficial and even vapid.

What we need are participarts.

XXII.

A participart is a participant in art. I don't think we
need audience members any longer. Participarts will
suffice.

Artists, curators, art historians, musicologists,
gallerists, dramaturgs, and cultural center administrators,
for example, must become participarts.

People may think there are only three dimensions to
art: the interaction of the artist, work-of-art, and audience
member. I've charted almost 50 dimensions of art (and that
is another book for another time.) In addition to artist,
work-of-art, and audience member, there are pre-work, co-
work, post-work, learning, conversation, and connection.
That's nine dimensions right there.

The participart adds substance, impact, and
endurance to an artistic encounter. The participart learns
and grows from the artistic encounter. The encounter is not
something to do; it is not playing badminton for five
minutes and the chomping on a Twinkie. It is emotional-
cognitive life, a solid workout, and good nutrition.

A participart engages the spectrum of the arts --
from the shiny object and blockbuster to regular concert or

exhibition; from the amateur to professional; from the old to the new.

A participart *is the* **something more** -- the enthusiasm that adds stability to an arts organization; allows an artist to make a living with art; that allows experimentation, celebration, and prosperity in the arts.

XXIII.

A participart in the Red Door realm will participate in the Usage Fee Philanthrophy™ projects such as Artober Caucus, other Badges of Meaning offerings, and Adrian's Day: Arts & Humanities Day.

XXIV.

Red Door is an "if you build it, they will come" project. "If you build it..." comes from W.P Kinsella's novel, "Shoeless Joe," in which an Iowa farmer builds a baseball diamond on his farm to coax the ghosts of scandalized baseball players back for one more game. The outfield borders a cornfield. This story was made into a movie, "Field of Dreams;" and as the baseballs step out of the corn, one asks, "Is this heaven?" To which the actor Kevin Costner asks, "No, it's Iowa."

Like many places, Iowa has real-life "if you build it, they will come" stories. When a couple wanted to donate their fantastic art collection to the University of Iowa in the 1960s, they included a caveat. They would donate their collection, if the university would build a museum for it. And build a splendid museum the university did.

Red Door aspires to be another real-life "if you build it, they will come" project with first phases funded by participarts and Usage Fee Philanthrophy™.

XXV.

The original Red Door has three parts.

The first part is *red dor,* Phase 1. I have the art of over 300 artists. These prints, photographs, sculptures, ceramics, and mostly paintings I'll use as pigments/found objects to create *red dor,* a 6,000-square-foot living, interactive, evolving, communicating, connecting, destination *p*Painting.

red dor will be a tourist attraction, eventually at the intensity of a secular pilgrimage. This tourism dynamic will help fund the operation of both *red dor* and Red Doors and move the Red Door project away from the fundraising mechanism. And tourism will only be one of many revenue streams for the Red Door Project.

Though *red dor,* Phase 1 will not create the full 6,000-square-foot tourist destination, it will provide a physical space to protect the integrity of the art and give a glimpse as to what *red dor* can be like.

The second part is the physical headquarters for the original Red Door headquarters. This space will serve as the figurehead, braintrust, and laboratory for the Red Door Project. As such, it will be a surprisingly small footprint and campus (one building.)

The growth of Red Door will be the partner sites in neighborhoods around the country; and these sites will be owned by community members in those neighborhoods.

The third part is the endowed directorship for Red Door. By having an endowed position, the payroll for the project's lead cheerleader is ensured and all the director's energy can be put into getting the Red Door project off the ground and generating a diaspora (the affiliate Red Doors) of neighborhoods that are being enriched with opportunities for informed civic dialogue, personal enrichment, and community building.

XXVI.

Who can provide the best home for the inaugural
Red Door?
These might be some leading contenders?

Iowa City, Iowa
Hills, Iowa
Cedar Rapids, Iowa
Dubuque, Iowa
Clinton, Iowa
Bellevue, Iowa
Lansing, Iowa
Winona, Minnesota
Ottumwa, Iowa
Newton, Iowa
San Antonio, Texas
Pittsburgh, Pennsylvania
Borough of the Bronx, New York
Minneapolis, Minnesota
Braddock, Pennsylvania
Maquoketa, Iowa
Davenport, Iowa

Detroit, Michigan
Prague, Czechia
Amsterdam, The Netherlands
Leeds, England
Chicago, Illinois
Glasgow, Scotland
Germany
France
Bratislava, Slovakia

Any community, large or small, could make its pitch for the original Red Door. If Phase 1 funding moves quickly, Red Door could start almost anywhere. But if Red Door or one of the Red Door affiliates starts on a shoestring, a community that could add a lot of vegetables and meat (if desired) to the soup could quickly establish itself as a front runner.

XXVII.

For a community interested in being the home for the inaugural Red Door or one of the first affiliates, the more of these ingredients it can provide, the better:

◆ a suitable building in need of a little TLC on a lease of $1 per year for ten years

◆ municipally-provided utilities, cable, and wifi for at least three years

◆ a good public transportation infrastructure

◆ annual public transporation pass for director for three years

◆ copious bicycle trails

◆ modest, suitable director housing on a lease of $1 per year for ten years

◆ municipally-provided utilities, cable, and wifi for this housing for at least three years

◆ public indoor swimming pool with copious hours dedicated to lap swimmers

◆ annual passes to recreation center with indoor running track and also to indoor pool mentioned above for director for at least three years

◆ two laptops and one desktop computers -- muncipally-provided and upgradable -- on leases of $1 per year for ten years

◆ local thought leader organizations willing to participate in the ongoing Red Door project and operation

◆ local media (print, television, radio, blog, social media) willing to participate in the ongoing Red Door project and operation

◆ local trade organizations and student classes willing to collaborate on the renovation and upgrades of the Red Door facility and director's residence

◆ options to purchase facility and residence at initial assessor's evaluation anytime within the ten-year period

◆ 10% of community members annually willing to be participarts in Artober Caucus

◆ 40% of community members willing to partake in at least one Red Door offering annually

A community thats offer much or all of the above list would be an attractive suitor to get the Red Door headquarters.

XXVIII.

Phase II of the Red Door Project is the underwriting of the endowment for the directorship.

XXIX.

Phase III of the Red Door project is to create the physical, full-blown home for *red dor*, the 6,000-square-foot destination and living *p*Painting.

XXX.

Phase IV of the Red Door Project will be the creation of the first three Red Door affiliates located somewhere in the country. These will likely be a bit more expensive than affiliate rollouts to follow as they will be pioneering, experimental pilots.

XXXI.

The four phases of the Red Door Project may cost:

Phase I:	$800,000
Phase II:	$3,000,000
Phase III:	$1,200,000
Phase IV:	$3,000,000

XXXII.

In the last few election cycles, presidential candidates, Democrat and Republican, and not even the frontrunners, have been able to raise millions of dollars not just in a quarter but in a weekend!

For 2020, because of an incumbent president, there was not a lot of caucus and primary activity on the Republican side. But there were almost thirty significant-weight candidates on the Democrat side. There were so many candidates, one debate had to be split over two nights.

Parameters were put into place to winnow participants for the debates. Candidates had to demonstrate, as one parameter, they had so many unique donors. The unique donor threshold (UDT) started at 50,000 and ended at 225,000. Candidates would ask people just to donate a dollar, so they could be counted toward the UDT. Of course, most people donated much more than a dollar.

(The Democratic leadership structure eventually dropped the donor requirement so Michael Bloomberg could participate.)

For the last debate before the February 2020 Iowa caucuses, five candidates had qualified for the debate -- Joe Biden, Pete Buttigieg, Amy Klobuchar, Bernie Sanders, Tom Steyer, and Elizabeth Warren. Though Cory Booker and Andrew Yang did not meet polling parameters to be part of the debate, they had attracted at least 225,000 unique donors.

Seven candidates attracted at least 225,000 donors. That is 1,575,000 donors. (Of course, many of these donors donated to multiple campaigns.) If each of these donors only gave the minimum dollar, that would be $1,575,000. If each of these donors averaged $10, the money raised by the politicians collectively would have been $15,750,000.

We are aiming for $6 average contributions, which would be $9,450,000.

Actually, our ambitions are even more modest. We would like to get 225,000 art-loving, conversation-loving, community building Democrats and 225,000 art-loving, conversation-loving, community building Republicans to give $6. That is 225,000 X 2 X $6 or $2,700,000.

$2,700,000 would pay for 100% of the first phase of the Red Door Project and 63% of the second phase.

And this $2,700,000 can be raised in a day!!!

(Of course, if 1,575,000 donors of all political spots and stripes donate $6, we could fund all four initial phases of the Red Door Project in one day!!!)

This is the premise of Artober Caucus -- not a political caucus but an art caucus -- an event which could raise at least $2,700,000 for the Red Door Project in 24 hours.

(We would like Artober Caucus to be an annual event. Until we get the first four phases of the Red Door

Project funded -- especially the first two phases -- we may run Artober Caucus monthly.)

I hope you will be the something more and financially support the Artober Caucus.

XXXIII.

Red Door is a community center, a common space, an art gallery, a gathering spot, a watering hole for the thirsty, a cafe for the hungry, a citizen, thought leader, and neighbor.

Red Door is a sacred space for meditation, reflection, and self-care; so Red Door is neighborhood catalyst.

Red Door is an entrepreneurial/artepreneurial emporium.

Red Door is not a politician but it is a soapbox.

Red Door is not a school but is a site of learning.

Red Door is not a hospital but it is a place of healing.

Red Door conversation and connection.

Red Door is meaning, mattering, purpose, and belonging.

Red Door is friend, family, home, enlightenment, and transcendence, so Red Door is cosmic third place.

Red Door is all of the above, so Red Door is MetaHouse.

And if you build it people will be able to come.

XXXIV.

 The Red Door Project will form a symbiotic relationship with Across the Fruited Plain, the initiative to form a polynodal cultural substrate (with, eventually, at least five nodes per state) which will nourish vibrant and integral artistic threads in communities all over the nation. Like Red Door has the funding mechanism, Artober Caucus, to help it germinate, the cultural substrate will have the funding mechanism of Adrian's Day: Arts & Humanities Day.
 You can read about the cultural substrate in "Across the Fruited Plain."

XXXV.

The Participart, the successor to spectator and audience member, will drive a new and potent thread to bring prosperity and vitality to the arts and humanities. One day, participarts will be understood as a concept and as a practice. But for now, my following obtuse descriptions may help you. Anyway, I hope you will become a participart and support Red Door. When you do, you will certainly become a champion of the arts.

Participarts are citizens in the world's first artistic nation; circulatory and nervous systems for vibrant creative and critical thinking communities enriching the larger communities.

Participarts know that engaging the arts is like exercise -- much more than entertainment, escape, diversion or something to do.

Participarts understand that engaging the arts in some capacity daily is as essential as good nutrition, exercise, learning, conversation, and social connection.

Participarts comprehend humans emerging from their capacities for imagination, abstraction, and storytelling, making the arts the prerequisite way of human knowing.

Participarts consider the arts as concentrated, impassioned, and dedicated inquiry, investigation, and reflection; so participarts utilize the arts as incredible wellsprings of insight and perspective that are inexpensive and accessible resources for communities and individuals on a daily basis.

Participarts realize the arts are much more than decoration, beauty and pleasing thoughts; the arts are consideration and conversation and exploration and they put us in the ever-ready-state of dialogue, engagement, reckoning, learning, storytelling, meaning-making, understanding, and enrichment. That is the arts' beauty.

Participarts recognize that the arts cannot be engaged sporadically and superficially no more than exercise, to benefit, can be engaged sporadically and superficially. Participarts recognize there are over 50 dimensions to an artistic encounter and they earnestly try to engage at least seven of those dimensions -- the 7-spot Crown -- as the take insight from the arts and put it into the practice of daily life enrichment.

Participarts offer a little something more to enhance the impactful life of arts events in their community. Participarts are the connective tissue that make the arts thrive at prosperous and sustaining levels in the community.

XXXVI.

Patrick Muller (ze/hem/hir) was born in Washington, Iowa, United States and came of age in Olomouc, Moravia, Czech Republic (now Czechia.) Ze attended undergraduate and graduate school at the University of Iowa (Iowa City, Iowa) and medical school at the Faculty of Medicine, Palacky University (Olomouc, Czechia.) Ze had a distinguished career in student service, higher education administration, and medical/dental educatizon.

e is the author of Healthcare Communication: A Rhetorical Handbook and, under the pseudonym belfort wunder, I can cure your cancer with this poem.

Hir proudest achievements were designing a standardized patient program for a college of dentistry; teaching interviewing, interpersonal, and physical exam skills to scores of dental, medical, and physician assistant students; and volunteering for fifteen years at a free medical clinic.

Ze became a self-taught artist, Hanpo, creating red dor as well as writing the books Continental Living Room and Across the Fruited Plain.

Now ze turns his attention to hir second career --
pPainter, artepreneur, and community builder -- with hir
role of executive director for Red Door.

And always ze remains mentor, student, explorer,
collaborator, neighbor, and friend.

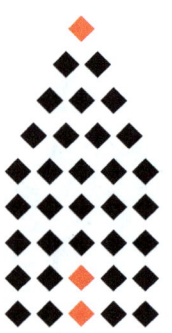

www.ingramcontent.com/pod-product-compliance
Lightning Source LLC
Chambersburg PA
CBHW070406220526
45467CB00001B/494